Underneath a Stranger Sky

Bethany Barnes

BookLeaf Publishing

India | USA | UK

Presentation by *BookLeaf Publishing*

Web: www.bookleafpub.com

E-mail: info@bookleafpub.com

ISBN : 9789357448406

First edition 2021

DEDICATION

To my love, for believing in me.

PREFACE

Not all stories have to be told as epic tales. Sometimes, when reading the tales of characters going on epic journeys, I find myself wondering what I would do. It's hard to believe that I would be in the forefront of great fights. What would I do if I was lost somewhere far away? How strong would my resolve be, how far could I go? I wanted to explore that here. A change of pace from the ever so popular heroes and their merry band of well-trained companions.

What would be the next step, if suddenly one found oneself in a new world?

Beginning

Sitting on the couch
Nothing but the sound of the dishwasher and a
car alarm in the parking lot
Surrounded by stacks of books and odd little
things.
You don't know how your friend convinced you
to do this
You're not even into witchcraft or astrology
You don't even believe in ghosts
"It'll be fine," they reassure you,
"I've done this a bunch of times–
Nothing really ever happens."
But you have this feeling
This cold pit in your stomach
Making your palms sweat and your throat go dry
You're not sure if this is a good idea anymore.

They light a candle.
The chanting starts
They're reading from a book with leather
covers,
Inscriptions scrawled on the side,
You're not sure if it's Latin or something made
up
But they're reading.

Eyes glazing over as they chant faster and faster
They have to be doing this from memory
There's no way they can read that fast.

A wind picks up
What's going on here?
The flame on the candle dances undisturbed
But your hair is flying around you
Whipping your face and tearing at your clothes.
What the hell?
"Stop it!" you shout, jumping up
Into the circle
"This isn't funny, stop!"
But they don't hear you
The wind is too strong, you cover your face
Doubled over from the force of it
Trying to stay upright.
Suddenly
It stops.

Change

"I'm never doing that again."
It's been a full minute since the wind stopped
You couldn't do anything but try to catch your
breath
And fix your hair into a bun because there was
nothing left to do with it.
Your friend had collapsed on the ground;
They didn't move for a moment
A heartbeat of terror
Then a groan.
"What the hell was that?"
Demanding, crossing the inscription on the
ground
Pulling them up to better yell
You didn't like this joke.
Their head rolls back
Out of focus at first and then blinking rapidly
They push back
Staring at the… sky?
Fear in their eyes
You realize you're not inside anymore.
What's going on?
You look up.

Two moons.

Closer than you have ever seen one
Taking up almost half the night sky.
Gentle light reflecting in a crescent phase,
Two Cheshire smiles in the dark,
Surrounded by stars in ways you've never seen
before.

You look back to your friend–
Your friend looks back at you–
Past each other, beyond the surrounding field
There was a forest where there wasn't one
before.
The top of a mountain in another distance;
You live in Kansas,
There are no mountains in Kansas,
Nothing higher than an anthill.
"What did you do?"

Shock

"I don't know."
The only words they seem to remember.
Not where they were,
Not what did they do,
Not what kind of sick joke is this,
What kind of drugs did you slip me–
I told you I wasn't into this sort of thing!
Can't you say anything else?

"It's not cold."
They were right.
Past the chill of the disappearing wind
It was warm,
Too warm for the thick jacket
Meant for January frost.
You're sweating profusely
But couldn't tell because you were too busy
shouting
My god, it's so quiet when you stop shouting…
Too quiet.
No crickets, birds, or the sound of car alarms,
There were no cars.
Besides the stars and strange glow on the
horizon
The only light was from the candle

Still dancing to no wind.

You take a long step back,
Slowly turn in a complete circle
Really hoping this is some sort of drug;
A shared trip, that's a thing, right?
There's no way this can be real.
The forest on one side, the far-away mountain
on the other.
In the distance, far enough you didn't see it at
first,
But close enough that you could clearly make it
out–
A house.
Something rustled on the edge of the forest.
Jumping, your friend snaps out of their trance,
Wild eyes and hyperventilating.
"Snap out of it!
You did this, you get us out of this."

"But I don't know how?"
Figure it out.

But it's too dark,
You can't read the book
And the rustling comes back.
You need shelter.
"Come on, we're going to the house."

Shelter

That was more than a mile
You'd think being in Kansas would teach you
how to judge distances.
Two hours, maybe three
The darkness only got deeper,
But the candle was still lit
And the feeble light was barely enough to tell
what was at the next step.
So you'd take one more step
And then another,
Stumbling through the uneven terrain
Hoping that whoever was in that house would
be…
Amenable.

The heat had lessened.
The pale glow on the horizon must have been
the sun
Going down to leave you both in darkness
Among the strangeness of the stars.
Spots of sticking sweat turned into points of
chill.
A wind picked up
Nothing like before, more gentle but still slightly
tugging at the clothes,

Sending shivers
It was the cold making you shake, right?

Your friend won't stop talking,
Promising you that they had no idea this would
happen,
Not knowing that the book was real magic.
Magic?
They had been working through the spells
But never had all the markings right,
Or all the…ingredients.
This was the first time.
They had done extra research to show off;
It was supposed to be fun.

Finally, the light from a glassless window shone
only feet away.
The house was wood,
Simply built, lumber
Hewn from hands, not something you'd find
among the mobile homes.
Who was going to knock?
You think they owe you that much,
You weren't keen on a gun in the face
From a paranoid stranger.

You blow out the candle.

Welcoming

"Who is it?
Visitors, travelers it seems,
A little late to be knocking on doors, don't you
think?"

"Look at them shiver!
Let them in by the fire
Nothing wrong with sharing a good meal and a
roof
You won't be causing any trouble will you?
My, you're so young."

Lit by a fire under a bubbling pot,
The room was nice,
Rustic like an old country home
Bare chairs around a small table
And a woven rug on the floor.
It smelled like leeks
And dirt
But that might have come from you.

"Come in now!
Don't want the draft bring us a cold
What strange clothes you have.

Not from around here are you?"

"No."
All you can muster.
You touch the door on the way in…
It's real.
You're starting to think this isn't drugs.
"Sorry, we're lost."

"I can see that from the way you have no packs.
Come sit by the fire, let me get you something to
eat.
You know, you're not the first to come knocking
on our door.
Seems to be the place
For strange young people."

They had not been the first?
How often does this happen?
"It's been an age
Many strange things had happened since.
Some good, some bad
But the others had never returned."

"You'll need to go to the Haven.
They can help you more than we can,
But the way is dangerous at night
Here, sleep by the fire."

Morning

Sleep did not come easy
Even though your feet hurt from walking so far,
And the shock of this new world exhausted you,
You found yourself staring into the burning
embers
Wondering, Wondering.

You wake with a start
Unsure of where you are
Or what woke you.
Looking around you remember:
Last Night,
The Book,
This Place.
Your friend is sound asleep beside you,
Curled on the rug under a blanket given by the
old couple.

"Didn't sleep well?"
Coming from the only other door in the home,
In the gloom you could barely make out their
shape
The windows were shuttered.
"Let me get you something to eat.
You have a long journey ahead of you."

Your friend wakes up from the sound of the
voice
Bleary eyed and face dimpled with marks from
the book's cover.
"What do you mean, long journey?"

"The Haven," they reply,
"It is a safe place,
Full of learning and magiks like yours,
It's where anyone with those abilities goes.
Naturally, you belong there."

Naturally?
It made sense,
Being unnatural here,
Even though the couple looked like ordinary
people
You wonder how different are they?
What could be waiting for them at the Haven?
Answers, hopefully.

Onset

They gave each of you a pack,
Small canvas totes with bread and wrapped
foods,
Some coins for bedrolls,
Small silver things with holes in the center,
And markings, not in a language you knew.

"Follow the road until you meet the mountain;
The city will be beyond the bend
There you should find better help."

The road, only a dozen feet away.
If only you had turned left last night
You could have walked on packed dirt instead of
an uneven field.
It makes you chuckle,
The only thing you could do with how
Ridiculous
All of this was.
What were you? Some grand adventurer?
This isn't what happens in real life.
You wonder if your parents worry.
You've been gone longer before
But never so far away.

Four days, they said,
Four days on foot
If you didn't stop at the town the road ran
through.
But it would be best
To get better clothes
Or at least ones that aren't as different.
People may ask questions
And some did not like travelers
From far away lands.

Walking

It was hot.
The dry sort of swelter that doesn't seem to
move.
The sun, massive but not as bright as you're
used to
Beating down heat;
You wish for some wind
Or a hat.

You're glad now that you wear neutral colors.
The loose grey shirt and denim pants,
Though showing your favorite band,
Seemed to blend in better with the surroundings
Than your friend's black and and blood red
outfit
And the chains around their neck.

The first day not a soul passed by
Rustling creatures in the grass were the only
company
And the dust kicked up from every step
Until it coated you up to your knees.
You really wished you had better shoes
These were not made for walking so far.

Your friend keeps thumbing through the pages of
the book.
The level ground makes it easier to walk and
read
But they can't fluently read Latin,
Or whatever language it really was,
They could only pick out bits of meaning
But nothing helpful.

"Will you shut up already?"

You had it with the mumbling.
You hadn't said anything to them since pointing
out the house
Frustration finally boiled over.
How could they get you into this mess?
And how are you getting home?
"I said I was sorry,"
They tried to count the excuses as such,
Not really knowing what they had read
Wasn't a good enough reason.
"We'll get out of this,
We'll be home soon. I promise.
We'll get to the Haven and they'll know how to
help."

But wasn't it strange?
They weren't the first to come here,

That's what the couple had said,
So what happened to the others?
Did they have the same book?
Did they ever make it home?
Something was wrong
More than being in the wrong world.

The Town

You didn't talk for the rest of the day;
By nightfall you found an outcropping of rocks
Some had littered the fields to your right during
the day
But these seemed large enough to shelter from
too much wind.
It had started again.
You didn't know how to build a fire
Sitting in the dark, eating little of the food,
Afraid that you'll run out too soon,
Huddled together for warmth,
Even with the jackets there was little comfort
Thankfully there were no flies.

Morning and you're stiff and hungry.
A little more bread, you wish you had water
Maybe you'll find a stream today.

You realize you've never had to walk all day
before.
Your feet hurt, blisters showing on the smallest
toes
From the look on your friend's face they feel it
too;

Next time they ask for a midnight adventure
You're telling them to f- off.

The sun wasn't as hot
Or the wind was stronger
It didn't matter as long as it felt nice.
Half through the day you could see the town
Far in the distance
But you could make it,
Hopefully sleep in a bed
Or at least under a roof.

The closer, the stronger the smell,
Rotting things and waste,
You cover your nose at first
Wondering how no one else seemed affected.
There were more people here
And many stared
Asking questions with their eyes,
Talking amongst themselves,
You couldn't make out the words
Whispered conversations just out of hearing.

The Innkeeper

An inn
Or at least what you would imagine one would
look like,
A raven with open wings
Standing on a nest as the sign
Slowly swinging over the doorway.
The air smelled like stale beer.

"Not many travelers pass by here,"
The innkeeper with rough hands
Wiping on a stained apron greeted.
"Though, you don't look much like travelers."

"We are on our way to the Haven, we need a
room for the night."

"Aye, it's certain you do."

You feel careful eyes watching from over their
mugs.
The innkeeper takes a long look at you
Nods his head to a side door
"You'll need better clothes than these."
As soon as the door is closed,
He opens a trunk at the foot of the bed

Filled to the top with clothes
And boots.
God those boots look comfortable.
"Not all are friendly to those who seek the
Haven.
You're lucky, a dear friend of mine was from
there
Had me keep this for anyone like him
Find what you will, but leave your clothes
behind
I'll get you food when you're done."

The door closed.
"How many others do you think there are?"

"I don't know. It's strange though, right?
What will we find when we get there?"

"Better yet, can anyone read that book?"

Cover

It felt like being in a renaissance fair-
Trousers and leather boots.
You kept the socks and underwear though,
No one would be able to see it anyway.
You traded your grey band shirt
For a full sleeved and slightly browned one
And a vest filled with pockets,
Bracers with leather straps,
And a traveling cloak.
You always read the characters wore those.

Your friend kept the chains
But tucked them away in the tote.
"Could be useful for later."
They're not wrong.
Unsure of what to do,
You fold your old clothes into the chest,
Emptying the pockets,
Luckily you had brought a lighter
And a small pocket knife
Though not much in the way of cigarettes here
You're rationing your sticks of gum.

Rest

Hot soup waited.
Beer and bread on a table away from the rest.
You pull your cloak closer
Trying to disappear away from the questioning
eyes.
You forget as soon as you start eating
Thick with potatoes and vegetables
Delicious, but could use some pepper.
The beer, watered down,
But for the better
You're thirsty
And never drank much beer.

The barmaid came by,
Kind smile on her mouth,
Curiosity in her eyes
Replaced the empty mugs with full beers.
Winking, either at you or your friend
Of something secret shared.

The inn filled, then emptied again,
The smell of beer was stronger
But it kept away the smells from outside.
You and your friend barely talk
Watching, like in a movie,

The men coming in from a hard day's work
Drinking and talking and sometimes singing,
One filling up a little too much
He fell out the door, missed the first step
The rest burst into laughter.
You couldn't help but grin.

The barmaid finally moved you away,
Back down a hallway of rooms to one emptied.
Two beds, thankfully,
Filled with straw and topped with blankets and
an old pillow.
You wonder for a moment about lice
But you're too tired to care
And fall asleep without getting undressed.

The Dream

A flash of light
A face, leering at you
Out of the darkness and so close.
I see we have another,
Younger this time,
How interesting that is
I wonder, what have you brought me?

You jump awake.
Light streams through the window
Nearly blinding, directly across your face,
You turn, you friend is awake too
The same look on their face.
"Did you have a dream too?"

Breakfast was agitated
Nervous, but it was only a dream right?
Two days in this strange place
You're bound to dream about something weird.
But sharing the same one?
Maybe you just had too much beer.
The innkeeper sat with you at the end
Wiping his hands on the apron,
At least it looked cleaner than yesterday.

"Look, it might be only two days
But the journey can be dangerous.
Be wary of strangers
Some aren't as kindly as I.
Here, hunting knives
Best for cooking and saving your skin
Go on, take them."
Carefully, you take one out of its sheath
Jagged teeth looked razor sharp,
As long as your forearm,
Slightly bent in halfway down.
You hope you won't need to use it
But loop the sheath through your waistband
Now it's starting to feel too much like a quest.

"Some dried meat and bread for the road,
A few apples as well,
And a waterskin.
There's a creek just inside the treeline,
Don't be going days without it again
You'll never make it that way.
Keep your head down,
And look like you know where you're going
Remember what I said about strangers
And good luck."

Continuing

You're glad you kept your socks
The boots were on the big side
Sliding on your heels as you walked down the
dusty road.
Otherwise, they were surprisingly comfortable.

You can't help but grin as you look over at your
friend,
Dressed in true fashion,
Some epic hero with dirt on their face
A bit of a scowl, but you think it might be a
hangover
The sun seemed brighter than yesterday.

"How many others do you think there were?"
You had been walking in silence most of the day
Mulling over what the innkeeper said
And the dream.
The question tugs at you
It felt like there was a secret that everyone knew
but you two
Something good or bad, you couldn't tell.

"I don't know, but enough to be known.
Maybe not normal

But the couple said it had happened before.
Something big must have happened
For the innkeeper to have all that ready.
I wonder who his friend was."

"Maybe we'll meet them at the Haven."
Maybe…maybe.
You're not sure what you're expecting,
Will there be a library?
A church?
You hoped not some satanic cult
If that book brought you here
Who knew what was waiting at the end of the
road.

Strangers pass by on carts,
Farmers going into town,
Traders leaving to the next,
A lone horse rider with his hood over his face.
None of them pay any mind
It was just two more people
They didn't look any different anymore.
It was comforting
The eyes from the night before had put you on
edge,
At least now you weren't being watched
Or the source of whispers.

Origins

Near sundown, after finding a sheltered spot by
the creek
Under trees with leaves larger than you've seen
before
You sit, drinking from the rushing waters
Hoping it won't make you sick.
Your friend is reading the book again,
Or trying to,
Piecing together words and phrases
Trying to find something helpful.
You doubt anything in there will help.

"Where did you get that?"
You don't know why you hadn't asked before.

"It was my grandad's,"
Surprised at the sudden question
They shut the book, and started to think.
"He said he's had it since he was a kid.
His friend, he got it from a pawn shop,
One of those voodoo places ya know?
Barely cost a nickel.
He had a friend then that liked that sort of thing.
He said his friend tried to take it
But he didn't want to give it away--"

Blood drains from their face
It was like looking at a ghost.

"What? What is it?"

Their voice cracked,
Barely a whisper above the sound of the creek,
You have to lean in to make out the words.
Visibly shaking, they continue:
"He had let his friend copy some of the pages.
One night his friend wanted to show him
something
But he felt odd, didn't like whatever it was
His friend went anyway…
They didn't come back the next day.

He was never found."

Distress

You couldn't sleep that night.
A chill, not from the wind
The hairs on your neck stand on end
The rustling leaves,
And sounds of unknown creatures,
Crept through the night
Just out of sight.

Morning dawned, none too soon.
You both eat in silence
Wondering the same thing.
Grandfather's friend,
Did they use the same spell?
Are they here now?
Is the Haven where they live?
What will you find there?
Will there be help?

Stiff again,
Joints creaking in the rapidly warming air,
You continue on.
Today would be the day for answers
You hope.
The trees are growing closer to the road now,

A thick forest on both sides,
The mountain towers above you now, blocking
nearly half your vision.
The road finally begins to bend
And the creek, joining a shallow river,
Bends with it.

The City

The sun is past midday
When you first see the city.
Built with its back to the mountain
So close for a moment
You think it was carved from the base.
But no
A high wall wraps itself around the city's base
Ending along the mountainside
And the river runs through it.
That must be the Haven.

Sitting on a log
You watch and try to see more clearly.
The jutting towers
And domed roofs
Reaching up from behind the city wall.
More people pass you now,
On business to or from the stone edifice,
None pay you mind
Past a glance, a wandering eye,
Curious about your friend picking through the
book again.

"Won't you put that away?"
You're tired of seeing it,

Of the frustrated sounds your friend made
As they try to decipher something.
Anything.

"Wait, I think I have something,"
They mark something in the dirt
You reach to stop them
But see that it's not in the book's language.
They're translating…
A letter here,
Part of a phrase,
It almost starts to make sense.
"See?"

Return —-- place belong
Therefore --------------Under sky
Stars -------conquer truth
And you —

"That could be it!"
You're hopeful too,
But scared,
Worried that whatever you're missing
Could bring something worse.

"We should wait," you say,
"They'll know how to read it
And we still have to see
If your grandad's friend came here too."

Stranger

"That's not a good idea."
You hadn't noticed
Someone had come out from the forest
Behind you.
You jump,
Grabbing the hunting knife.
Shaking, your friend doing the same,
Pointing at a man
Much older than yourself.
Old enough to be your father,
But covered in strangely sewn clothing
Bits and pieces in a patchwork.
But unarmed,
Thankfully.

"Peace, friends,"
He puts his hands up,
Calloused palms facing you
At level with his deep set eyes
And shaggy brown hair
"I mean you no harm."

"Why sneak up on us?
Why were you listening?"
You still don't lower your knife

The last traveler had passed by minutes ago
Their back to you and not likely to help.
"Who are you?" you demand.

"I am like you," he says,
Pulling back a sleeve
To show a tattoo
Of…AC/DC?

Your arm falls
Oh my god.
You hear your friend's knife fall to the ground
Is this real?
"I'm here to save you," he says.

Warning

"What…happened?"
You gesture to his being.
The twisted beard,
The row of knives on his belt,
The weathered features on his face.
"How long have you been here?"

"It's hard to tell," he says,
"The years work differently here
And they're shorter than years
On Earth.

"But I had gotten a copy of this book,
Something handwritten I found
Looking around an abandoned house.
I was a photographer
And I like taking pictures
Of old things.

"Anyway, I had learned latin back in school
And it seemed like directions to
'A Place Unknown to Earth.'
It sounded cool,
And I was young,
So I tried it out."

He stopped for a moment,
Blinking back tears.
You don't understand.
What's wrong?

"I was told to go to the Haven,
That someone was there that could help.
Turns out I wasn't the first one
So I went.
I had barely gone in the gates
When an old woman pulled me aside,
Told me to run,
I wasn't safe there.
Later I learned that someone…
Also from Earth…
They kidnapped them all.
None of the others ever leave the city
Or are seen again."

Fear

What happened to the others?
He's not sure,
But knows there's some dark magik.
The person behind the walls
Either kills or uses the others
Maybe trying to get back home
Or trying to get stronger.

A storm was brewing;
Magik users from around the known world
Building fortresses.
Some joining the man behind the wall,
Some building to keep him out.
Rumor said he was looking for something:
A book,
One he thought the other travelers would bring
with them,
But they never had one
At least by the time they arrived.
It was a book of spells,
Including the one
That sent him here.

Stunned silence
What do you say?

What could you do?
This place was dangerous.
More dangerous than you had imagined…

"We have to get out of here."

9 789357 448406